A captain before he was 21; a household name throughout most of Europe at 39; killed in action just after his 47th birthday; Nelson lived a colourful, crowded and short life. He masterminded some of British history's most resounding victories – at the Nile in 1798, Copenhagen in 1801 and Trafalgar in 1805 – losing an arm and the sight in one eye in the process. He also had a tempestuous and very public love affair with Emma Hamilton, one of the most beautiful women of her day.

Affectionate, engaging, a devoted friend and father, he was also ruthless and occasionally even cruel. Uninspiring and less than heroic in his personal appearance, he was still one of Britain's most charismatic leaders, able to inspire devotion, even love, in those who served with him.

It is this combination of opposites that makes Nelson so fascinating: there is always something new to be said about him, some new insight into his complex character. Thanks to discoveries by many researchers at the time of the bicentenary of the Battle of Trafalgar in 2005 we now know more than ever about the real man – his precise role in his most significant battles and the conduct of his closest relationships. This small book, drawing on the Nelson exhibitions and collections at the National Museum of the Royal Navy, Portsmouth, offers a brief introduction to the story of the man who is still widely regarded as one of Britain's greatest heroes.

Left: 'The Battle of Trafalgar', by Thomas Luny (1759–1837).

THE BOY, 1758–1779

'What has poor Horace done, who is so weak
... that he should be sent to rough it out at sea?'

Letter from Captain Maurice Suckling, 1771

*H*oratio Nelson was born on 29 September 1758 in the small village of Burnham Thorpe on the north coast of Norfolk. His parents were Catherine and Edmund Nelson, the latter being the parish priest, and in many ways his childhood was unconventional. His mother died when he was nine – a psychological blow which left a permanent scar – and then, in March 1771, aged only 12, he joined the Royal Navy under the patronage of his uncle, Captain Maurice Suckling, and was away from home for most of his teens. Overall, he was a bright, engaging little boy who constantly sought attention and approval from adults and was naturally impulsive, especially in his affections. These two strands run right throughout his life and provide the underlying pattern to all his actions, public as well as private.

Even in the Navy his training was unconventional. Captain Suckling seems to have deliberately planned for the young Horatio to enjoy as wide a variety of experience as possible. After a short spell in the Thames estuary in his uncle's ship, the 64-gun HMS *Raisonnable*, he made a voyage to the West Indies in the merchantman *Mary Ann*. Then, still aged only 14, he took part in an expedition to the Arctic and finally completed his early training with a two-year stint in the crack frigate HMS *Seahorse* in the East Indies, which is where he saw action for the first time. He then fell dangerously ill with malaria and had to be invalided home in 1775. Even so, his first four years in the Navy had been packed with activity and had given him a wide range of experience, in different types of ship and different environments, which helped to nurture his natural independence and energy.

Having recovered from his illness, Nelson passed his lieutenant's examination on 5 April 1777. After he'd served just a year in the frigate HMS *Lowestoffe* on the West Indies station, her captain, William Locker, gave him command of a small schooner that acted as the frigate's tender. Less than a year later he was promoted to commander and was given his first independent command, the brig HMS *Badger*, and six months later, in June 1779, he received the key promotion to post of captain, when he was still three months short of his 21st birthday. Promotion this rapid was not as unusual as some have suggested in the past, but it was nevertheless impressive.

Left: The Parsonage, Burnham Thorpe. Nelson's childhood home was pulled down in his lifetime, but this near contemporary painting gives a good idea of what it looked like.

Above: Notes written by Edmund Nelson on, 'Horatio, My Third Son' in 1781.

'I am so very uneasy ... having just receiv'd the Account of the death of my dear good Uncle whose loss falls very heavy on me. His friendship I am sure I shall always retain a most grateful sense off. Even in his illness he did not forget me but recommend'd me in the Strongest manner to Sir Peter Parker who has promis'd me he will make me the First Captain ...'

(Letter to his father from HMS *Bristol* in Port Royal Harbour, Jamaica, 24 October 1778, following the death of Captain Suckling)

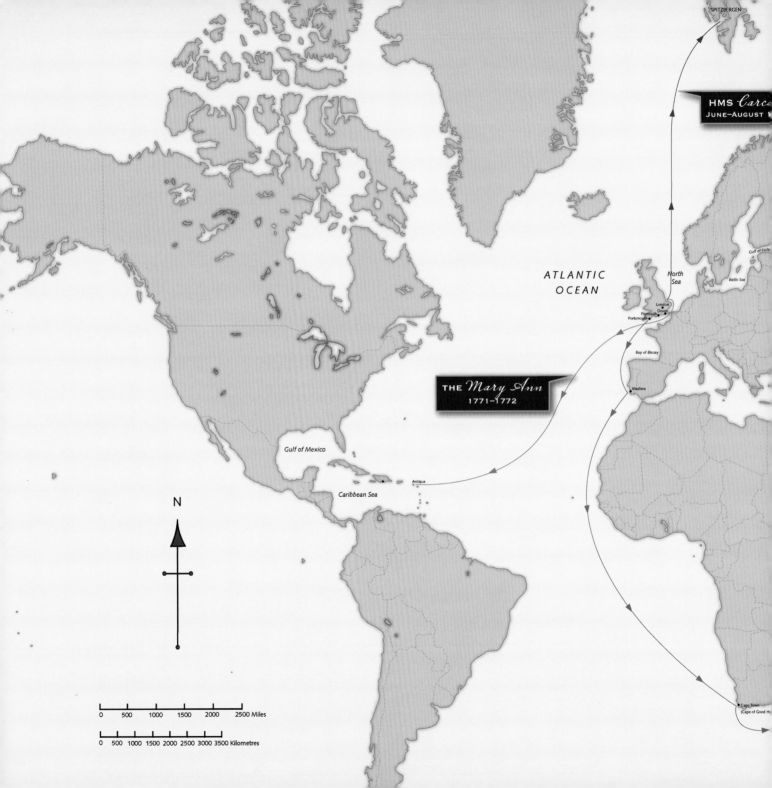

ATLANTIC
OCEAN

SPITZBERGEN

HMS *Carca*
JUNE–AUGUST

North
Sea

Gulf of Finla

Baltic Sea

London
Dover
Plymouth
Portsmouth

Bay of Biscay

Madiera

THE *Mary Ann*
1771–1772

Gulf of Mexico

Antiqua

Caribbean Sea

Cape Town
(Cape of Good Ho

N

0   500   1000   1500   2000   2500 Miles

0   500 1000 1500 2000 2500 3000 3500 Kilometres

Left: Nelson's early voyages. By the age of 16 Nelson had already sailed many 1000s of miles at sea from the Arctic to the Bay of Bengal.

East China Sea

South China Sea

Arabian Sea

Bombay

Calcutta

Bay of Bengal

Madras

Trincomalee

INDIAN OCEAN

HMS *Seahorse*
OCTOBER 1773–MARCH 1776

THE FRIGATE CAPTAIN, 1780–1793

'Our admiral is tolerable, but I do not like him, he bows and scrapes too much for me ...'

Letter to William Locker, HMS *Boreas*, English Harbour, 24th September 1784.

Left: Captain Horatio Nelson, Francis Rigaud (1742–1810), 1780.

Following his promotion, Nelson spent eight years almost continuously in command of frigates: the *Hinchinbrooke*, the *Albemarle* and finally the *Boreas*. Until 1783 Britain was at war with her American colonies in the American War of Independence; more seriously, she was also fighting the fleets of the French and Spanish, who had entered the war on the colonies' side. There were a number of major fleet actions and most of Nelson's naval contemporaries served in the battle squadrons, whilst he by contrast took part in only one action. In 1780 he was involved in the small-scale river-borne attack on the Spanish Fort San Juan in modern-day Nicaragua, following which he suffered a second bout of sickness that kept him out of active service for almost a year.

His next peacetime appointment, in command of the frigate HMS *Boreas* in the West Indies between 1784 and 1787, was not successful. Nelson became involved in a dispute over illicit trading between the British colonies and the newly independent American states and created powerful enemies among the rich British traders and senior officials in the area. He also mishandled a delicate situation involving Prince William Henry, a son of King George III who was in command of the frigate HMS *Pegasus*. When the Prince had a disagreement with his first lieutenant, William Schomberg, Nelson failed to defuse the potentially embarrassing incident and allowed the Prince to flout naval rules, earning the displeasure of the Admiralty and, indeed, of the King himself. At this point his career faltered and almost ended. Between 1788 and 1793 he was unable to get any naval employment, despite repeated requests.

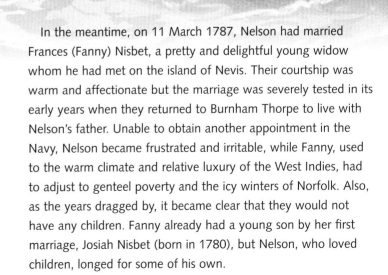

Right: A Royal Navy frigate at sea. As a young captain Nelson gained long experience in command of frigates, and grew accustomed to making independent decisions.

Below: On their marriage Frances Nesbit was just 26 but had already known Nelson for 2 years. She had first married at the age of 18 but had been widowed 2 years later. Her son Josiah was already 7 and would go to sea with Nelson in 1793. This water-colour from 1798 is the earliest known image of Fanny.

In the meantime, on 11 March 1787, Nelson had married Frances (Fanny) Nisbet, a pretty and delightful young widow whom he had met on the island of Nevis. Their courtship was warm and affectionate but the marriage was severely tested in its early years when they returned to Burnham Thorpe to live with Nelson's father. Unable to obtain another appointment in the Navy, Nelson became frustrated and irritable, while Fanny, used to the warm climate and relative luxury of the West Indies, had to adjust to genteel poverty and the icy winters of Norfolk. Also, as the years dragged by, it became clear that they would not have any children. Fanny already had a young son by her first marriage, Josiah Nisbet (born in 1780), but Nelson, who loved children, longed for some of his own.

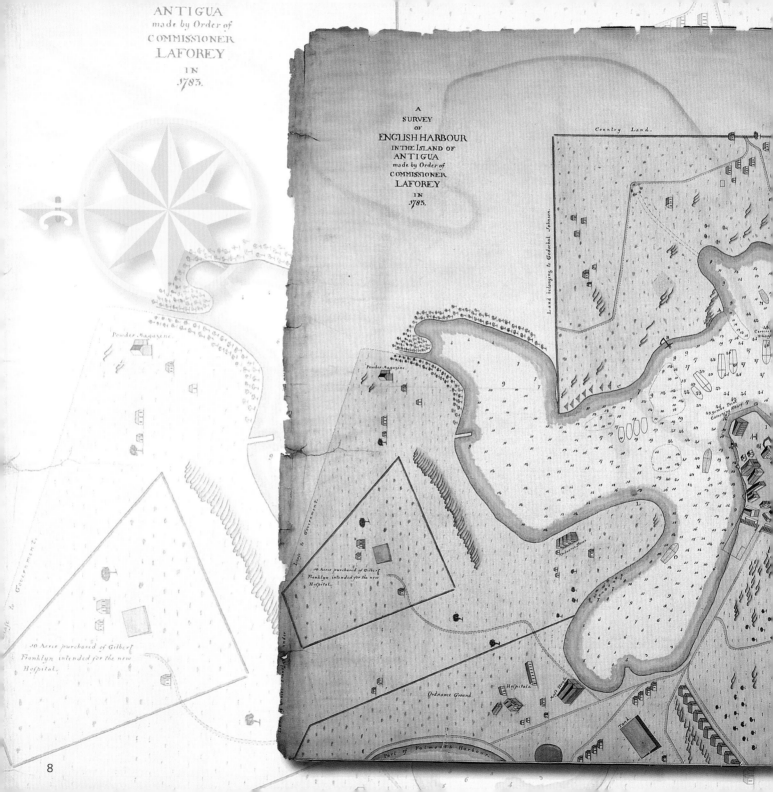

ANTIGUA
made by Order of
COMMISSIONER
LAFOREY
IN
1783.

A
SURVEY
OF
ENGLISH HARBOUR
IN THE ISLAND OF
ANTIGUA
made by Order of
COMMISSIONER
LAFOREY
IN
1783.

Country Land.

Land belonging to Godschal Johnson.

Powder Magazine.

Powder Magazine.

Land to Government.

50 Acres purchased of Gilbert
Franklyn intended for the new
Hospital.

50 Acres purchased of Gilbert
Franklyn intended for the new
Hospital.

Ordnance Ground

Hospitals

Part of Falmouth Harbour

8

Left: English Harbour, Antigua in 1783. During his command of HMS *Boreas*, English Harbour provided an essential safe anchorage and base to clean and re-supply the ship and crew. It was also close to the island of Nevis where Frances Nesbit lived.

THE BATTLESHIP CAPTAIN, 1793–1796

> 'After clouds come sunshine. The Admiralty so smile upon me, that really I am as much surprised as when they frowned ...'
>
> Letter to his wife, London, 7th January 1793

Nelson's six years of inactivity ended in February 1793 when war broke out with revolutionary France and he was offered command of the 64-gun battleship HMS *Agamemnon*. Having gathered a ship's company, including a large hand-picked contingent of men from Norfolk, he sailed to join the Mediterranean fleet, under Admiral Lord Hood. So began an important stage in his career, one which gave him experience of independent command when he took important operational decisions by himself.

In 1794 Hood gave him command of naval forces ashore during the capture of Corsica, and he was present at the siege and capture of the two key towns Bastia and Calvi. At Calvi he lost almost all sight in his right eye when he was hit in the face by gravel thrown up by a French cannonball; thereafter the eye was only able to distinguish light from dark.

In 1795 he had a brief spell with the main fleet, by then commanded by Admiral William Hotham, and for the first time took part in two fleet battles. At the Battle of the Gulf of Genoa (13/14 March 1795) he showed his independent spirit by taking the *Agamemnon* to attack a disabled French ship, the *Ça Ira*. He dealt the much larger ship and her crew such a heavy blow that she fell an easy prey to the British when the fighting resumed the next day, but was furious when Hotham ended the action after only two prizes had been taken.

Above: Nelson at the Siege of Calvi, 12 July 1794. A pen and wash painting by William Bromley shows Nelson when struck in the face.

He was then detached to the Mediterranean coast of Italy as a commodore in command of a small squadron, with which he assisted the Austrian army in its fight against the victorious French armies under the rising new general Napoleon Bonaparte. He put in place a tight blockade of French-held ports, and in 1796 organised the capture of the islands of Elba and Capraia. He also found time to take his first mistress, the opera singer Adelaide Correglia, whom he met in Leghorn.

In these years his exploits won Nelson the regard of a number of influential people – notably the First Lord of the Admiralty, Lord Spencer, and the new commander-in-chief in the Mediterranean, Sir John Jervis. But, despite the approval of such men, he began to feel that he was not sufficiently appreciated in Britain. His letters to his wife and family at this time are full of complaints that his actions had not been publicly recognised or rewarded. Fortunately this was about to change.

Above right: Nelson visited Toulon whilst it was occupied by the Royal Navy in 1793. Here is the arsenal burning as the Navy withdrew.

Right: Nelson's squadron manoeuvring at the Battle of Genoa, 1795.

Below: 'The Launch of the Agamemnon, 1781, Buckler's Hard' by Harold Wyllie.

'None since Lord Howe's Action can lay claim equal to Me, five actions in my Ship 3 at Sea 2

agt: the Walls of Bastia, 2 sieges & three boat fights are my Claim & annexed to the hardest Service of any Ship this war.'

(Letter to his Norfolk friend the Revd Dixon Hoste after the Battle of Genoa, 2 April 1795 from St Fiorenzo)

THE BATTLE OF CAPE ST VINCENT, 14 FEBRUARY 1797

> To receive the Swords of the vanquished, on the quarter-deck of a Spanish first-rate, can seldom fall to the good fortune of any Man ...'
>
> Letter to Gilbert Elliott, HMS *Irresistible*, 16th February 1797

Above: Deck of the San Josef.

*E*arly in 1797 France and her allies planned a major invasion of British-held Ireland, backed by their fleets. Their opening moves were countered and thwarted by Sir Admiral John Jervis's remarkable victory over the Spanish fleet at the Battle of Cape St Vincent, in which Nelson played a decisive role.

Historians' accounts of the battle have tended to portray Nelson as the lone genius who saved the day by his unconventional approach. However, the truth is more complex and it is now clear that Jervis himself handled the battle unconventionally right from the outset. First he formed his ships into a loose line of battle and drove swiftly for a gap in the Spanish line. Then, having split the enemy fleet into two unequal groups, he ordered his own fleet to attack the larger group in three divisions.

A fierce melée ensued, in which a number of Spanish ships suffered badly from the fast and accurate British broadsides. Two of them, the San Nicolas and the San Josef, while trying desperately to get out of range, collided and became entangled. Seeing this, Nelson ordered the Captain to be placed alongside the San Nicolas and then personally led a boarding party to capture her. The San Josef, which had already been badly mauled by gunfire from other British ships, began firing on Nelson and his party in an attempt to assist their comrades. So he duly led his men up the sides of the larger ship and captured her as well, becoming personally responsible for taking two of the four prizes that were won in the Battle.

It was a remarkable feat, unprecedented in naval history, and Nelson was deservedly the hero of the hour. He received a gold medal from George III and was made a Knight of the Bath, with the right to wear a distinctive star on his uniform coat and to style himself 'Sir Horatio Nelson'. The public recognition he had craved was his at last.

"A soldier of the 69th regiment having broke the upper quarter-gallery window, jumped in, followed by myself and others as fast as possible. I found the cabin doors fastened, and some Spanish officers fired their pistols; but having broke open the doors, the soldiers fired, and the Spanish Brigadier fell ... I believe, we lost about seven killed and ten wounded, and about twenty Spaniards lost their lives by foolish resistance.

(From 'A Few Remarks Relative to Myself in the Captain ...' signed by Nelson and two captains, 1797)

Above: This print shows Nelson's captures during the war, including the San Josef and San Nicholas with their Spanish flags top right.

Right: 'NELSON'S PATENT BRIDGE'. Nelson's feat at St Vincent, when he captured the San José by boarding her from the decks of the San Nicolas, was nicknamed 'Nelson's Patent Bridge for Boarding First Rates'.

SANTA CRUZ DE TENERIFE, JULY 1797

'... a left-handed admiral will never again be considered useful ...'
Letter to Admiral Sir John Jervis, HMS *Theseus*, 16th August 1797.

Following his success at Cape St Vincent, Admiral Jervis sent Nelson to attack Tenerife in the Spanish-controlled Canary Islands. Nelson planned the operation carefully but all his preparations were frustrated by a factor beyond his control – the weather. Contrary winds and currents prevented his landing force from reaching their objective, and when they did manage to get ashore the Spanish were organised and could not be dislodged from their strong defensive positions.

At this point Nelson received intelligence that the Spanish had very few professional soldiers and were in a state of disarray and confusion. At a council of war with all his captains, he was urged to attack again and needed little persuasion. As the British sailors and Royal Marines stormed the town jetty and citadel, they were cut down by concentrated fire – and Nelson himself had his upper right arm shattered by a musket ball. A few small parties managed to struggle ashore and barricaded themselves in a monastery, but they were surrounded and cut off from their comrades and eventually agreed to surrender. The attack was a disaster that lost Nelson almost a quarter of his force in killed and wounded, the worst defeat of his career.

Luckily his stepson, Josiah Nisbet, was at his side in the boat and saved his life. Nisbet staunched the flow of blood from the dangerous wound and then managed to get Nelson back to his flagship, where the arm was amputated. Not unnaturally, Nelson was very depressed – both by the large number of casualties and by the blow to his own future prospects. As he wrote in a letter to Jervis, '... a left-handed admiral will never again be considered as useful.'

Jervis was sympathetic and sent Nelson to Britain to recover. The arm took a long time to heal, but Nelson recorded how one day he awoke after an unusually sound sleep to find that the pain had suddenly disappeared. The loss of his arm involved changes in Nelson's life – most obviously for historians the switch to left-handed writing. There were alterations to his clothes: the empty sleeve was pinned across his chest; specially shortened right-arm sleeves were made for his shirts; breeches, stockings and shoes were worn instead of boots.

'Sir, I cannot depart from this Island, without returning your Excellency my sincerest thanks for your attention towards me, by your humanity in favour of our wounded men in your power, or under your care ... P.S. I trust your Excellency will do me the honour to accept a Cask of English beer and a cheese.'

(Letter to the Commandant-General of the Canary Islands from HMS *Theseus*, opposite Santa Cruz de Tenerife, 26 July 1797)

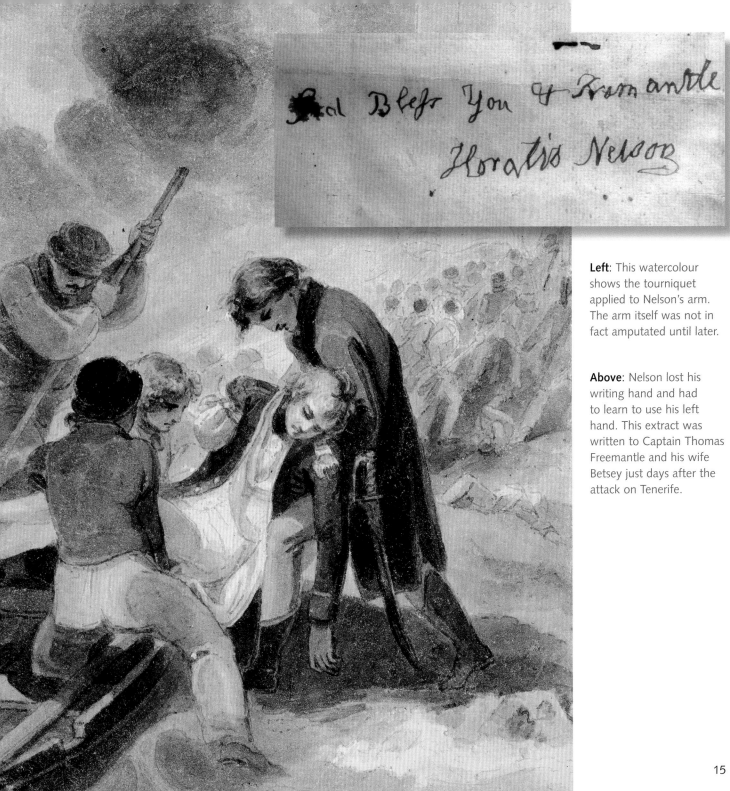

God Bless You & Fremantle

Horatio Nelson

Left: This watercolour shows the tourniquet applied to Nelson's arm. The arm itself was not in fact amputated until later.

Above: Nelson lost his writing hand and had to learn to use his left hand. This extract was written to Captain Thomas Freemantle and his wife Betsey just days after the attack on Tenerife.

THE NILE CAMPAIGN, JUNE–SEPTEMBER 1798

'We few, we happy few, we band of brothers ...'
King Henry V, Shakespeare

On rejoining Admiral Lord St Vincent's fleet in May 1798, Nelson was immediately despatched into the Mediterranean with 14 battleships commanded by some of the most experienced captains of the fleet. Their mission was to find and destroy a significant French expeditionary force, known to be at large, under the overall command of General Napoleon Bonaparte.

After only a year as an admiral, and aged just 39, Nelson now found himself with a level of responsibility that would have taxed an older and more experienced man. He rose to the challenge superbly. After a long and frustrating chase he tracked the French fleet down in Egypt, finding them at anchor in Aboukir Bay, to the east of Alexandria, on 1 August 1798.

Nelson's battle plans had been agreed with his captains some time before. As a result, having made the decision to attack at once, even though night was falling, he was able to leave the detailed conduct of the action to his subordinates. As the British fleet sailed headlong into the Bay, Captain Foley, in the leading ship HMS *Goliath*, noticed that the French had left enough room at the head of their line for him to round their van and attack on the landward side. His bold initiative was followed by the ships astern of him until Nelson, arriving in his flagship HMS *Vanguard*, began a second attack on the seaward side. So, right at the outset, the French van was overwhelmed, crushed on

Left: This brilliant caricature by James Gilray depicts Nelson wielding his cudgel of 'British Oak' to attack the French ships (red, white and blue crocodiles). The exploding crocodile to the rear represents the L'Orient.

Above: 'The Band of Brothers'. Nelson used this phrase to describe the very close professional relationship he enjoyed with the captains that served with him at the Battle of the Nile. It comes from his favourite Shakespeare play, King Henry V.

Above: The news of victory at the Nile was celebrated more widely than any other of Nelson's victories.

both sides by superior numbers and firepower. Crucially, since the wind was blowing directly down their line, the rearmost ships were unable to do anything to help their comrades and were forced to wait helplessly as the battle rolled towards them. Eventually, 11 out of the 13 French battleships were captured or destroyed, including the massive flagship *L'Orient*, which blew up at the height of the battle.

Nelson was wounded when a piece of shrapnel struck him on the forehead, causing a flap of skin to fall over his good eye. Blinded with blood, he thought at first the wound was mortal and collapsed into the arms of his Flag Captain Edmund Berry saying, 'I am killed. Remember me to my wife.'

The Battle of the Nile is now generally regarded as Nelson's most decisive victory, surpassing even Trafalgar. Nelson became an international celebrity as soon as the news reached Europe, and for the rest of his life he was known as 'The Hero of the Nile'.

Right: The magazines on the French flagship L'Orient exploded at about 10 pm with devastating loss of life and a noise that was heard 10 miles away. Recent archaeological investigations have found debris hurled far from the main wreck.

NAPLES AND EMMA HAMILTON, 1798–1800

> **'O Nelson, Nelson! What do we not owe you!
> O Victor! Saviour of Italy!'**
>
> Emma Hamilton reporting the reaction of the Queen
> of Naples, September 1798

Following the Battle of the Nile, Nelson went to Naples to recover from his wound. He stayed with his friends Sir William Hamilton, the British Envoy, and his beautiful wife Emma. It was meant to be a short visit but, in the end, Nelson's close involvement with Naples lasted nearly two years. His actions there were controversial at the time and have remained controversial ever since.

He had a significant impact on Neapolitan affairs and gradually began to neglect his wider command. In 1799, when the French occupied Naples and established a republic, he helped the King to recover his throne, becoming directly involved in a very bloody and vicious civil war. He was personally implicated in some ugly incidents, such as the trial and summary execution of one of the republican leaders, Commodore Francesco Carraciolo, and of a number of other key Neapolitan revolutionaries. The debate about Nelson's complicity in these atrocities, and whether or not he should be held responsible for them, continues to this day.

At the same time, he fell in love with Emma Hamilton. She nursed him tenderly when he first arrived in Naples, sick and shaken with his head wound, and she was at his side throughout the events of 1799, when he was wrestling with the complexities of Neapolitan politics. In such an intense atmosphere it was, perhaps, not surprising that two such impetuous and impulsively affectionate people should become close friends, and then lovers. What is surprising is that they did so little to hide it. Recent research suggests that they probably did not start a physical relationship until late in 1799 – but long before then their public behaviour had already made them a rich source of gossip and scandal.

Sir William Hamilton has often been written off as a foolish old cuckold. However it is now clear that he knew what was happening but was content to ignore the affair in order to retain the companionship of his wife and the friendship of a man he regarded as a son. In his will he left Nelson a miniature of Emma '... in token of the great regard I have for His Lordship, the most virtuous, loyal and truly brave character I ever met with. God bless him – and shame fall on those who do not say, Amen.'

Opposite: Nelson's fleet at anchor in the Bay of Naples, by the Neapolitan artist Giacomo Guardi.

Below left: Miniature of Emma Hamilton. She was beautiful as well as a gifted actress and singer who spoke French and Italian fluently. Down to earth and enthusiastic, she never lost her Cheshire accent and so was regarded as 'vulgar' by the snobbish society she sought to enter, and by Nelson's 19th-century biographers, who tended – most unfairly – to heap all the blame for their affair on her.

Below centre: Miniature portrait of William Hamilton painted by Charles Grignon in Salerno, 1799. By this date Hamilton was 69 and had been Envoy to Naples since 1764.

Below right: Mourning locket containing hair of Prince Albert of Naples. Six year-old Prince Albert died in Emma Hamilton's arms on Christmas Day, 1798. The Royal Family were fleeing from Naples in Nelson's flagship, HMS Vanguard.

'On the 22nd ... the Royal Family of the Two Sicilies were safely embarked on board the *Vanguard*. Lady Hamilton ... every night received the jewels of the Royal Family and such clothes as might be necessary for the very large party to embark, to the amount, I am confident of full two million five hundred thousand pounds sterling.'

(Letter to Earl St Vincent from Palermo, 28 December 1798, describing evacuation of Naples)

FANNY, EMMA AND HORATIA, 1800–1801

'I have been the world around ... and never yet saw your equal ...'

Letter to Emma Hamilton, San Josef, 8th February 1801

The rumours about Nelson and Emma's affair had preceded them and Fanny Nelson had of course heard them. It appears that Nelson genuinely believed his wife would be prepared to remain as complacent as Sir William, so that the affair with Emma could continue. In fact, although Fanny was bewildered and upset by the breakdown of her marriage, she had her own brand of quiet and dignified courage, against which Nelson's ruthless eagerness beat in vain. In the end he was forced to choose between his wife and his lover, a decision that clearly wracked him with guilt.

Ultimately Emma had one great advantage over Fanny, for she knew, by then, that she was pregnant. The prospect of a child of his own at last made up Nelson's mind and the separation from Fanny that followed was cruelly decisive – and so swift that for a while she could not believe it had happened. She poured out her bewilderment, and her longing to win her husband back, in a moving series of letters to one of Nelson's friends, Alexander Davison, that were only discovered in 2001. However, Nelson was relentless, and having made a generous financial provision for her cut her out of his life and refused to see her, or even to communicate with her, again.

In early 1801 Nelson was summoned to serve at sea once more with the Channel Fleet. He was desperately unhappy at being separated from Emma, and his letters, which he wrote to her almost daily, reflect his emotional instability at this time. Worry about her pregnancy was followed by wild exhilaration

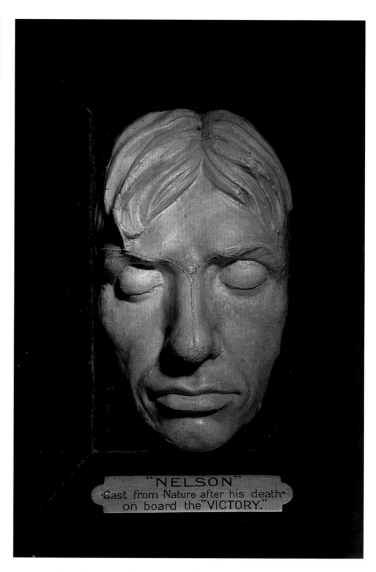

Above: This plaster mask is now in fact believed to be a 'Life Mask', cast from Nelson's face during his visit to Vienna in 1800.

when she gave birth to a daughter, Horatia. The child's existence had to be concealed, and the couple devised an elaborate charade so that they could write to each other openly about her. They invented a sailor on board Nelson's ship by the name of 'Thompson', who had a pregnant wife that was being looked after by Emma. Nelson then wrote letters to 'Mrs Thompson' apparently on the sailor's behalf, passing on tender messages of love to her and the infant.

Right: This cruel caricature 'Dido in Despair' imagines a fat Emma to be distraught at home as Nelson sails away.

Right: A silver cup given to his daughter by Nelson with the inscription, 'To my much loved Horatia, 21 August 1805'. It is one of many items in the Museum which were donated to the Museum by direct descent from Horatia.

'I have received your letter ... I only wish people would never mention my name to you ... I want neither nursing or attention. And had you come here I should not have gone on Shore nor would you have come afloat. I fixed as I though a proper allowance to enable you to remain quiet and not to be posting from one end of the Kingdom to the other.'

(Letter to Frances, Lady Nelson following their separation, 17 February 1801)

THE BATTLE OF COPENHAGEN, 2 APRIL 1801

'... I see no Signal ...'

*I*n early 1801 the Baltic states created the 'Armed Neutrality of the North' and placed an embargo on the trading of British ships. In response, a fleet was sent to the Baltic under the overall command of Admiral Sir Hyde Parker, with Nelson as second in command.

Negotiations with Denmark failed and Parker handed over the direction of offensive operations to his subordinate. The Danes had placed a defensive line of hulks and floating batteries in front of Copenhagen, to keep any attacking force out of bombardment range of the city. This had to be subdued – a task made more difficult by the shoals and forts protecting the flanks of the floating line.

Nelson was at his charismatic best, filling everyone with confidence, drawing up detailed plans to deal with the Danish line and then, finally, dining with some of his key subordinates to brief them and infuse them with his fighting spirit.

The ensuing British victory was very much due to Nelson's determination and refusal to be discouraged by mishaps. In the opening moments of the battle he lost a quarter of his attacking force when three of his ships got into difficulties with the shoals. He then found that the Danish resistance was stronger, and more prolonged, than expected. As the battle dragged on for longer than planned, Parker, watching nervously from a distance, sent a signal ordering Nelson to withdraw. Famously, Nelson claimed he could not see the signal and fought on.

About an hour later, sensing that the Danish line was beginning to give way, Nelson sent a message to the Danish

Left: Admiral Hyde Parker. When Hyde Parker ordered Nelson to retreat, Nelson is supposed to have placed a telescope to his blind eye and claimed he could not see the signal. This is the origin of the phrase 'turning a blind eye.'

Right: This music written by a naval officer once belonged to Emma Hamilton.

Left: This print shows just how close Nelson's ships were to both the defensive hulks and to the city itself.

Crown Prince offering a truce. By the time the Crown Prince received the letter, the centre of the Danish line had collapsed and the way was open for a British bombardment. He agreed to Nelson's suggestion and the battle ended.

Having begun negotiations, Nelson was encouraged by Parker to continue them. The Danes were on the point of agreeing to an armistice when news arrived that Tsar Paul of Russia, the main architect of the Armed Neutrality, had been assassinated. Denmark therefore felt able to withdraw from a confrontation with Britain that had never enjoyed popular support.

When news of the battle reached Britain, Parker was recalled and Nelson was appointed commander-in-chief. It was an important turning point in his career; he had shown that he was not just a brilliant fighting admiral but a skilled administrator and diplomat as well.

Sir, I believe I may congratulate Your Royal Highness on the recent success of our Incomparable Navy which I trust has not tarnish'd its ancient splendour. It was my good fortune to Command such a very distinguish'd sett of fine fellows, and to have the arrangement of the attack.'

(Letter to the Duke of Clarence two days after the Battle, dated HMS *St George*, 4 April 1801)

THE CHANNEL AND MERTON,
1801–1803

> 'Sir William died at ten minutes past ten, this morning, in Lady Hamilton's and my arms ...'
>
> Letter to Alexander Davison, 11 o'clock, 6th April 1803

When Nelson returned from the Baltic in early July 1801 he found the country gripped by an invasion scare. The Admiralty appointed him commander-in-chief of a large fleet of small vessels in the Channel, directed to defend the Thames Estuary and the south coast and to attack and destroy the French invasion forces. Nelson quickly realised that the invasion threat was a sham and that the move was essentially a public relations exercise, intended to calm public fears by placing the Hero of the Nile in the front line.

He did make one major attempt to attack the French forces in their harbours, at Boulogne on 15 August, but his opponent, Admiral Louis de Latouche Tréville, was an experienced commander who had studied Nelson's methods and made careful preparations to counter them. As a result, the British attack was repulsed with heavy casualties.

In early September 1801, as rumours of approaching peace with France began to circulate, Nelson pleaded to be allowed to relinquish his command, but his requests were firmly turned down. Eventually, however, at the end of October, the peace negotiations reached a point where the Government at last felt able to release him and he went to live ashore with the Hamiltons.

While Nelson had been at sea, Emma had found a house for him with a small estate attached at Merton, then a little village in Surrey. He purchased it, despite a very bad surveyor's report, with

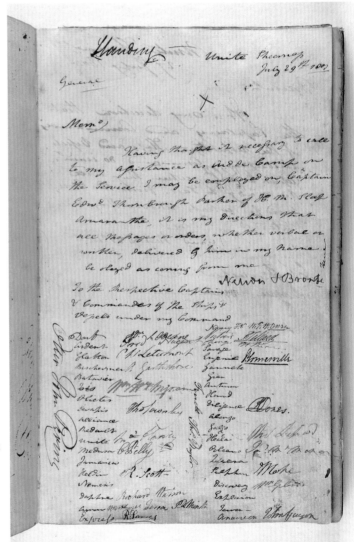

A Jig round the Statue of Peace, or All Parties Reconciled

Above: This caricature from 1801 shows Nelson and Napoleon hand-in-hand dancing a jig of peace.

Left: Nelson's 'Order Book' from the Channel. This was Nelson's largest command – he had over 100 vessels of varying sizes in his fleet in the summer of 1801. It was by far the largest force he ever commanded – for example at Trafalgar he commanded only 33 ships.

Below: Merton Place by Thomas Baxter. A watercolour painted after Nelson's death, but which gives a good impression of the house.

the help of a loan from his friend and agent Alexander Davison. For the next 18 months, he, Emma and William Hamilton often lived there together in a curious, but evidently very amicable, *ménage à trois*. It was an unusual and happy period of quiet retirement, broken only by visits to London to take part in debates in the House of Lords and, in the summer of 1802, by a protracted tour of South Wales and the Midlands. Planned as a private holiday, it quickly turned into a triumphant progress, showing Nelson at first hand just how popular he was with the ordinary people of Britain.

The Boats put off from the *Medusa* at half-past eleven o'clock last night, in the best possible order, and before one o'clock this morning, the firing began, and I had ... the most perfect confidence of complete success; but the darkness of the night, with the tide and half-tide, separated the Divisions; and from not all arriving at the same happy moment with Captain Parker is to be attributed the failure of success.'

(Letter to Secretary of the Admiralty, *Medusa* off Boulogne, 16 August 1801 following attack on Boulogne)

THE MEDITERRANEAN COMMAND, MAY 1803–AUGUST 1805

'I have hoisted my flag onboard his Majesty's Ship *Victory* ...'
Letter to the Secretary of the Admiralty, Portsmouth, 18th May 1803

When war with France broke out again, in May 1803, Nelson was given his most prestigious appointment – the command of the Mediterranean Fleet. He was to be away at sea for more than two years, but during this time he appears to have achieved a serenity in his relationship with Emma that had been lacking in the earlier years. His letters to her were calmer, even mundane, with none of the jealous anguish of those he had written in early 1801. Now he wrote to her as if they were

Above: Nelson's dramatic pursuit of Villenueve's fleet took him 1000s of miles across the Atlantic and back.

Above: The Admiral's Day Cabin.

If you can get my things onboard *Victory* pray lose no time part will be at Portsmouth. I hope that by the time you receive this letter that the Waggon will have arrived. Lord Gardner of course will give you Boats, if you can get 12 good Sheep some Hay and Fowls ... it will do no harm for I may get out in the *Victory* ...'

(A newly discovered letter written in haste and sent to Samuel Sutton, Captain of HMS *Victory*, from the Admiralty 17 May 1803, the day after the re-commencement of hostilities with France)

a married couple, with gossip about mutual friends, instructions about building projects at Merton and plans for Horatia's future.

These two years were a remarkable climax to his career. Nelson proved an excellent administrator: he kept his ships afloat and in fighting trim without any dockyard refits, and ensured his men were happy, healthy and well-fed. He ran a most efficient intelligence service, gathering and reporting information from all the corners of his command. He also displayed a sure diplomatic touch in his dealings with the many different countries bordering the Mediterranean.

Nelson still longed to beat the French one more time. Indeed, instead of blockading them closely in harbour, he constantly tempted them to come out by keeping the main body of his force well out of sight of land. The risk was, of course, that they might be able to escape without his seeing them – which is exactly what happened, twice, in 1805. In January the French admiral, Pierre de Villeneuve, managed to elude Nelson's watching frigates but was forced to return to port after encountering a heavy storm. In March he got clean away to the West Indies at the start of the grand campaign by means of which Napoleon hoped to unite his fleets with those of the Spanish and then bring them, a single large force, to the Channel to cover an invasion of Britain.

Nelson chased after him, and succeeded in driving the ships back to European waters before they could do much damage to the rich British possessions. Then he returned home to Britain for a rest after two years at sea, arriving at Portsmouth on 19 August 1805 only to find himself the man of the moment. Politicians, from Prime Minister William Pitt down, wanted to consult him and ask his advice, and whenever he appeared on the streets of London he was surrounded by cheering crowds. As he himself remarked ruefully, 'I am now set up for a conjurer.'

Above: Nelson in the Great Cabin on HMS *Victory*, by Charles Lucy.

TRAFALGAR 21 OCTOBER 1805

> **'... something must be left to chance in a sea fight ...'**
>
> Memorandum, HMS *Victory*, off Cadiz, 9th October 1805

The combined French and Spanish fleets had taken refuge in Cádiz and the Admiralty began assembling a fleet to deal with them. The command was offered to Nelson as a matter of course. Before he left Merton, he went with Emma to the parish church, where they took private communion and exchanged rings in a quasi-marriage service. They had had only 25 days together.

Nelson joined the fleet in HMS *Victory* off Cádiz on 28 September. Only a handful of the captains had served with him before and so he had to build a new band of brothers in a few days. The next day, his 47th birthday, he held a dinner party in the *Victory* at which he explained his plan for defeating the enemy – 'The Nelson Touch', as he called it. As at the Nile and Copenhagen, his aim was to bring overwhelming force to bear on one part of the enemy's line and to crush it as quickly as possible. To achieve this, he aimed to attack in two divisions, splitting his opponents' line into three segments. In a single phrase he summed up his leadership ethos: '… in case signals can neither be seen or perfectly understood, no captain can do very wrong if he places his ship alongside that of an enemy.' The man who had seized the initiative at Cape St Vincent eight years before was now empowering his subordinates to do the same.

The Franco-Spanish fleet sailed from Cádiz on 19 October 1805, heading south. Napoleon had now started a new campaign against Austria and had ordered the French admiral, Villeneuve, to sail into the Mediterranean in support. Nelson shadowed them until they were well clear of harbour and then, on the morning of 21 October, turned to attack. The battle unfolded very much as he had planned. One British division, under Vice Admiral Cuthbert Collingwood, enveloped the allied rear, crushing it with superior gunfire, while another under Nelson smashed through the centre of the allied line, cutting it in two and preventing the van from helping their comrades. Having led the way through a hail of shot, the *Victory* became entangled with a smaller French battleship, the *Redoutable*, and it was from her rigging that the bullet was fired which struck Nelson at about 1.15 p.m., as he was pacing the quarterdeck with Captain Thomas Hardy. Carried

down to the cockpit below the *Victory*'s waterline, where the wounded were treated in comparative safety, he lingered, in great pain, long enough to learn that he had won a decisive victory. His last words were, 'Thank God I have done my duty.'

Of the 33 French and Spanish ships that had begun the battle, 18 had been either captured or destroyed, four escaped only to be captured a fortnight later at the Battle of Cape Ortegal, and 11 managed to struggle back into Cádiz.

Opposite: The Battle of Trafalgar, by Nicholas Pocock.

'May the Great God, whom I worship, grant to my Country, and for the benefit of Europe in general, a great and glorious Victory; and may no misconduct in any one tarnish it; and may humanity after Victory be the predominant feature in the British Fleet. For myself, individually, I commit my life to Him who made me ...'

(From Nelson's private diary, 21 October 1805)

THE IMMORTAL MEMORY

Rejoicing at the remarkable victory at Trafalgar was overshadowed by grief at the loss of Nelson. Midshipman Joseph Woollnough of HMS *Agamemnon* recorded that when his comrades heard the news 'A stranger might have supposed from the gloom that spread among them that they had been beaten instead of being conquerors.' When the news reached Britain there was similar mixed reaction. Robert Southey, the Poet Laureate, later recalled in his *Life of Nelson*, published in 1813, that in Britain, 'The victory of Trafalgar was celebrated, indeed, with the usual forms of rejoicing, but they were without joy.' Nelson's body was brought home and lay in state in the Painted Hall in Greenwich Hospital before being transported to London in an elaborate river procession. It was then taken to St Paul's Cathedral where, after a spectacular funeral service, it was finally laid to rest in the crypt, immediately beneath the great dome.

Nelson's life and death were celebrated in a surge of heroic paintings, statues, poetry and popular art. Anything that had belonged to him was preserved as a sacred relic – from the bullet that killed him and the blood-stained coat he was wearing at Trafalgar to ordinary items such as his shoe buckles and handkerchiefs. Most macabre of all, his hair was cut off and distributed amongst his friends.

In a sermon preached on 5 December 1805, a special day of thanksgiving for the victory at Trafalgar, the Revd Thomas Wood said, 'His name is a monument that will exist undiminished throughout all ages and be warmly cherished in the remembrance of Britons.' Sure enough, more than two hundred years after his death, Nelson is still a popular British hero, surpassing all his contemporaries. Museum exhibitions examine his career, there is a constant public appetite for books about his life and times, whilst his famous flagship HMS *Victory* is preserved in the old Royal Dockyard at Portsmouth.

In October the Royal Navy still marks Trafalgar Day with special ceremonies and with formal dinners at which the toast is always drunk to 'The Immortal Memory'.